I made this book to show how much I love you!

To _ _ _ _ _ _ _ _ _ _ _ _

From _ _ _ _ _ _ _ _ _ _ _ _

My dad looks like this :

Our favorite thing to do together is

_____

_____

_____

_____

You are super awesome because you

_____

_____

_____

_____

The best thing about you is

_____

_____

_____

_____

You always smile when

_____

_____

_____

_____

A poem about
my dad

_____

_____

_____

_____

_____

_____

You are the happiest when

_____

_____

_____

_____

You are there for me when

_____

_____

_____

_____

My favorite memory of us

You taught me how to

_____

_____

_____

_____

We all had so much fun when we went to

_____

_____

_____

_____

I like it when you tell me that I am

_____

_____

_____

_____

Four words describe You

DAD

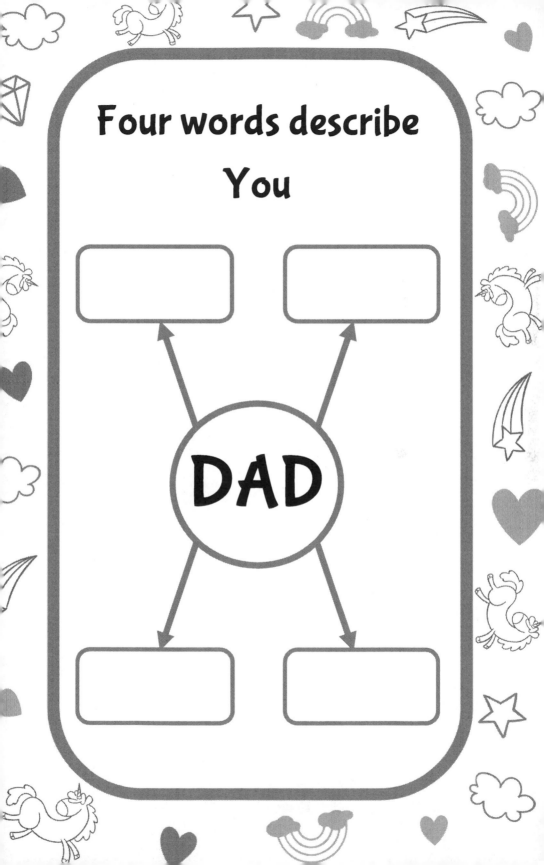

You make me laugh when

_____

_____

_____

_____

The funniest thing you do is

_____

_____

_____

_____

You always help me to

_____

_____

_____

_____

You are
good at

_____

_____

_____

_____

You are
smarter than

_____

_____

_____

_____

Your favorite food is

_____

_____

_____

_____

Movie/TV show that we both love is

_____

_____

_____

_____

I enjoyed a lot when we went to

_____

_____

_____

_____

I love you because

_____

_____

_____

_____

I 'm proud to say you are

_____

_____

_____

_____

Made in the USA
Middletown, DE
15 June 2023